Beyond Being Bullied

If you're reading this guide, it means you have some SUPER strength. It means you've overcome a bully. Some people think that people who are bullied are weak, but in fact, the exact opposite is true! Bullies act tough, but they're really the ones who are weak while people who overcome bullies are strong. As you complete the activities below, remind yourself that you're SUPER STRONG because you've overcome a bully.

Look at the chart below and read the feelings that are often attached to being bullied. In the blank circles, write some of the other feelings you had when you were being bullied.

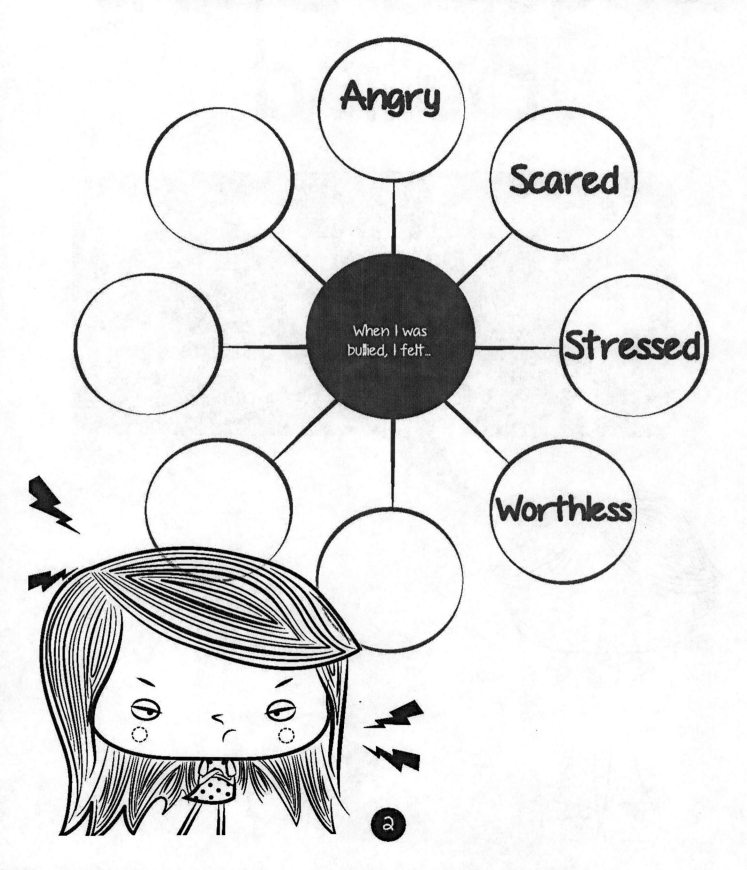

Angry

Scared

Stressed

Worthless

When I was bullied, I felt...

In the box below, draw a picture of how you felt about yourself when you were being bullied

On the ribbons below, write the qualities that make you a special and wonderful person.

I'm a good person because

You already drew a picture of yourself after dealing with a bully. Now draw a picture of yourself the way people who love you see you.

In the speech bubbles below, write something your bully has said or done to make you feel bad. In the thought bubble next to each, write a positive statement about yourself to beat that bad feeling down!

Bullies use their words (and sometimes fists) to make us feel bad. When others use words and actions to make us feel bad, we might start to believe them. But there are also people around us who offer compliments and tell us good things. Cross out each fist below to take away the bully feelings and write something positive others (friends, family members, teachers, etc.) have told you in the high fives. Circle the high fives to remember the wonderful things people see in you!

In each box below, write the name of a person who loves and cares about you.

In the box below, draw a picture of yourself achieving one of your greatest accomplishments.

Describe your accomplishment on the lines below.

Sometimes bullies make us feel small, but the truth is they can't stop us from growing big! In the box below, draw yourself as a grownup. In your drawing, describe the job you'd like to have and the things you'd like to accomplish.

My Bully

I went to school afraid today
Of what my bully might do or say.
I never know what to expect
Except that for sure my day will be wrecked.
My bully makes me feel unsafe
No matter how hard I try to be brave.
My bully makes me feel very small
Even though he isn't too tall.
My bully makes me feel really bad
And most of all, I feel super sad.
I used to look forward to going to school
That was before my bully broke rules.
I want to feel safe when I go to class
I want to feel happy without wearing a mask.
I think the best place to start feeling good
Is remembering why my mom said I should.
Picking on others is what cowards do
Standing up to a bully is how to stay true.
I will no longer let my bully make me feel bad
I will remember he bullies because he is sad.
Bullies are people who feel really weak
So they act super tough and not at all meek.
They pick out the strong kids to pick on instead
Of practicing strength in their own heart and head.

Underline/highlight the parts of the poem that apply to how you feel.

11

Part of overcoming a bully is understanding why they do what they do. In the chart below, one column lists reasons bullies hurt people. On the other side, write ways they can get these needs met without bullying.

Bullies hurt people because...	How bullies can do better...
1. They only feel powerful when they make others feel afraid.	
2. They think people will respect them if they're afraid.	
3. By putting others down, they feel better about themselves.	
4. They don't know how to make friends.	
5. Someone was probably really mean to them, and they continued the cycle by being mean to others.	
6. They don't want to be bullied by others, so they bully.	

In the boxes below, draw examples of ways to treat people with kindness. Then choose one of those ways to treat someone you know.

When you were being bullied, lots of things were probably running through your mind. Write some of those things in the thought bubbles below.

Bullies can rob us of our self-esteem.
Take it back by listing ten great things
about yourself.

1. _____
2. _____
3. _____
4. _____
5. _____
6. _____
7. _____
8. _____
9. _____
10. _____

 Color the star below, and write your name in the middle.

Draw a picture of a place where you feel safe at school.

On the lines below, describe why you feel safe in this place.

_____

_____

_____

_____

_____

Can you imagine how boring the world would be if everyone was exactly the same? In the diamonds below, write or draw things that make you unique.

Superheroes help defend others from bullies. In the box below, draw yourself as a superhero who deflects the negative effects of bullies.

One of the best ways to help yourself through hard feelings you have after being bullied is to help others who are going through it too. Draw a poster to show support for other kids who've experienced a bully.

On the lines below, write a letter to yourself, describing your best qualities and traits. Give yourself compliments and reminders of why you're special and how you overcame your bully.

Dear _____,

_____

_____

_____

_____

_____

_____

_____

_____

_____

_____

Love,

_____

Can you think of characters in books, movies, or TV shows who've been bullied? List them in the shapes below.

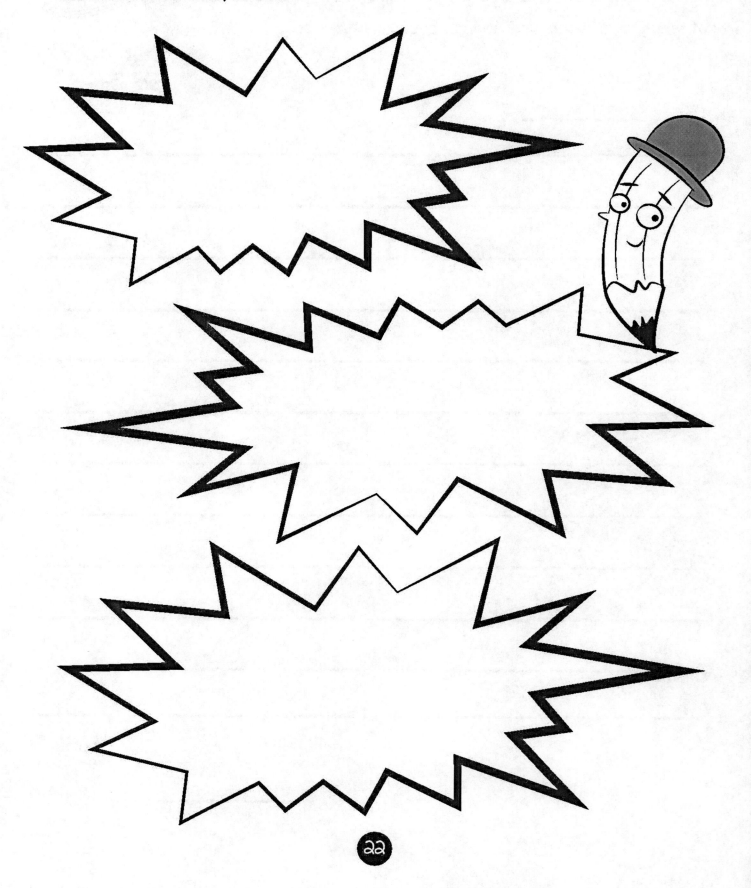

Now think of yourself as the star in your own story.
Write or draw your story in the shape below.

Overcoming a bully gives you strength that others can't take away. Write a list of the new strengths you have since overcoming your bully.

1. _____

2. _____

3. _____

4. _____

5. _____

6. _____

7. _____

8. _____

Draw your super-strong, anti-bully muscles in the box below.

The words bullies use are hurtful and can leave scars. Circle where the bully hurt you, and then write one positive thing about yourself on the circle to cover the scar the bully left.

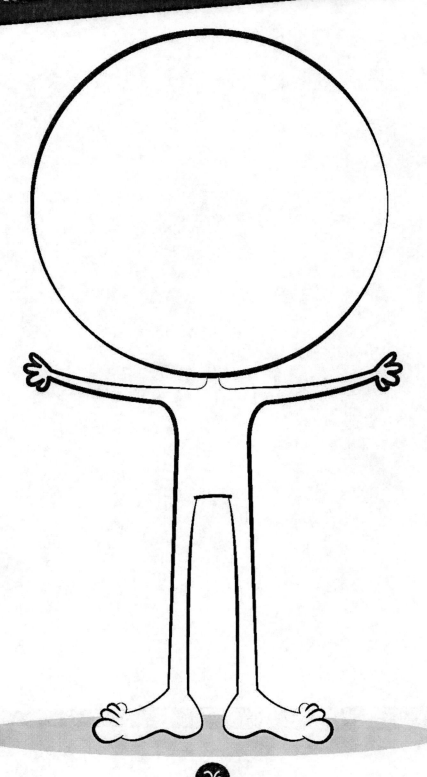

Write a letter to the person who bullied you. Write down EVERYTHING you have to say to the bully — let all your anger and hurt go so you're not holding it inside any longer.

Dear Bully,

_____

_____

_____

_____

_____

_____

_____

_____

_____

_____

From,

_____

When you're bullied, the bully can make you feel really small. In the first box, draw a picture of how you felt in comparison to the bully. Now that you're not being bullied, it's important for you to remember how strong and wonderful you are. In the second box, draw a picture of how you feel now or how you want to feel compared to the bully.

When being bullied

Now

Think of things the bully said to you that hurt. Write each of those things in the shapes below, then X them out. Don't allow the bully to hurt you with those mean words anymore.

Fill in the chart below with things you love to do. It's important to remember what you love to do and what you are good at. Try to do at least one activity from your chart every day!

Things I Love To Do

Sometimes it's helpful to know you're helping someone else. Since you've overcome being bullied, think about the advice you'd give to those who are being bullied now. Write each piece of advice in a bubble.

Everyone should have a support circle. You should have people you can talk to about anything. Those people love you for YOU! Create your support circle below. Look at it to remind yourself of the supportive people in your life.

Even after being bullied, you may still feel unsafe. That is a terrible feeling! Think about the places you feel safe, and draw pictures of those places in the boxes below. Whenever you're feeling unsafe, try to get to one of your safe places.

Make a list of ten things you'd like to improve about yourself.
These can become your goals of improvement.

Goals of Improvement

1. _____
2. _____
3. _____
4. _____
5. _____
6. _____
7. _____
8. _____
9. _____
10. _____

Become a Leader

You were a target of a bully. Now, think about what you can do to prevent someone else from becoming a target. Here is a list of things you can do to become a leader at your school, in your neighborhood, and in your community.

Get Involved:

1. Talk with adults at your school to inform them of where bullying is occurring. Oftentimes, adults do not really know where bullying occurs.
2. Create anti-bully posters to hang on the walls of your school.
3. Become a role model for younger kids.
4. Lead by example. Let others follow your example and create a positive impact on your surroundings.
5. Talk with your principal about creating an anti-bully club or group.
6. Be a part of the school safety committee or student council in your school. This will give you a voice where you can make a change in your school's climate.
7. _____
   _____
   _____

8. _____
   _____
   _____

Take Care of Yourself

Be kind to yourself. In the banners below, write down ways to be kind to yourself. You are AWESOME and you DESERVE to be treated with kindness and respect. Start by treating yourself with kindness.

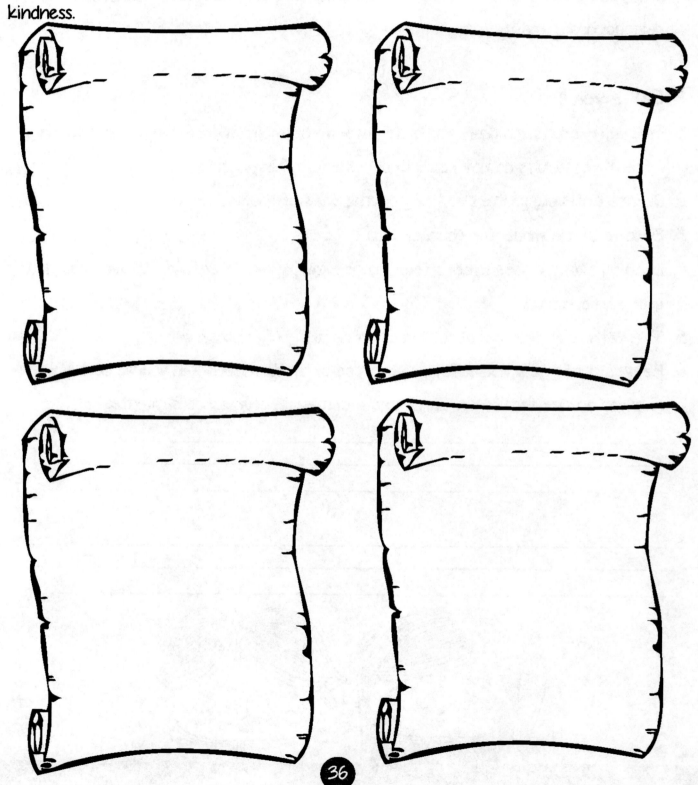

Now that you've described your super strength, awesome qualities, and supportive friends and family, what are some of the things you've learned about how to deal with bullies in the future? List them in the ovals below.

Beyond Being Bullied: A Resiliency Workbook for Kids Who Have Been Bullied

Text copyright © 2014 by Erainna Winnett, Ed.S.

Book Cover Design copyright © 2014 by Lucia Martinez

www.counselingwithheart.com

ISBN-10: 0615911781

BISAC: Juvenile Nonfiction / Social Issues / Bullying

Printed in the United States of America

CPSIA information can be obtained at www.ICGtesting.com
Printed in the USA
BVOW03s0540260515

401812BV00012B/16/P